WEAPONS AND MACHINES IN WARFARE

WEAPONS AND MACHINES OF THE COLD WAR

Craig Boutland

Cavendish Square

Published in 2024 by Cavendish Square Publishing, LLC
2544 Clinton Street, Buffalo, NY 14224

Portions of this work were originally authored by Charlie Samuels and published as *Machines and Weaponry of the Cold War*. All new material this edition authored by Craig Boutland.

Website: cavendishsq.com

Design Manager: Keith Davis
Picture Manager: Sophie Mortimer

Picture Credits
Front Cover: U.S. Department of Defense
All photographs U.S. Department of Defense Except: BAe Ltd: 20; Alan Denney: 34;
RIA Novosti: 43tr; Robert Hunt Library: 1, 9, 16, 21, 24, 28, 29tl, 31, 32, 43bl, 45tl; Shutterstock: Paul Drabot 18, Stephen Meese 45tr; Thinkstock: Hemera 35tl, iStockphoto 8.
Key: t = top, c = center, b = bottom, l = left, r = right.

Cataloging-in-Publication Data

Names: Boutland, Craig.
Title: Weapons and machines of the Cold War / Craig Boutland.
Description: Buffalo, New York : Cavendish Square Publishing, 2024. | Series: Weapons and machines in warfare | Includes glossary and index.
Identifiers: ISBN 9781502669148 (pbk.) | ISBN 9781502669155 (library bound) | ISBN 9781502669162 (ebook)
Subjects: LCSH: Cold War--Juvenile literature. | World politics--1945-1989--Juvenile literature. | Nuclear warfare--Juvenile literature.
Classification: LCC E744.B66 2024 | DDC 909.82'5--dc23

CPSIA compliance information: Batch #CSCSQ24: For further information contact Cavendish Square Publishing LLC at 1-877-980-4450.

Printed in the United States of America

CONTENTS

A Tomahawk cruise missile streaks away from USS *Missouri*. In the Cold War, long-range missiles were the most important form of weapon.

Introduction

World War II ended in victory over Germany in 1945. The victorious nations were soon in dispute, however. The United States and its allies believed in democracy and freedom of economic activity. The Soviet Union, which controlled much of eastern Europe, promoted communism—state control of the lives of citizens. This clash between the two **ideologies** is called the Cold War. It lasted from the 1940s until 1991.

ideology: A system of political ideas that forms the basis of a society.

U.S. military personnel watch a nuclear explosion in the Nevada desert in 1951. At the time, the dangers of nuclear **fallout** were not entirely understood, so the men are standing too close for safety.

IN THE SHADOW OF THE BOMB

The Cold War never erupted into open warfare between the two major powers. However, there were smaller wars in which each side tried to weaken the other by supporting and arming one set of combatants or the other.

The introduction of nuclear weapons in 1945 cast a shadow over the Cold War. A single atomic bomb could destroy a whole city. So-called strategic weapons such as submarines, missiles, and aircraft were kept in constant readiness so as to deter any sudden attack by the other side. The world lived in fear of a nuclear war for more than 40 years.

fallout: The spread of harmful microscopic nuclear material after an atomic explosion.

Smoke blasts from the back of a B-47 as it uses rocket power for a quick takeoff. The pods beneath the wings carried additional fuel.

B-47 Stratojet

Work on a new U.S. bomber had begun near the end of World War II. The idea was to design an airplane with jet propulsion that could fly from the U.S. to attack targets in Europe. The new aircraft was named the B-47 when it came into service. More than 2,000 were built. They carried **nuclear** bombs. They remained in service from 1951 to 1969.

nuclear: A bomb that works by releasing the vast power contained in atoms.

INNOVATIVE DESIGN

The B-47 flew at high altitudes at high speeds. This was thanks to its **swept wings;** straight wings would not allow the aircraft to use the full power of the engines. By the 1960s, most passenger planes had copied this style, and now it is the standard design.

The jet had a crew of three and a maximum speed of 607 mph (977 km/h). Its range could be up to 10,000 miles (16,100 km). As well as being a bomber, the B-47 could take photos, carry out electronic surveillance, and gather data about the weather. It was never used as a bomber in actual warfare, however.

EYEWITNESS

"I can't say enough good things about it. I loved it! I didn't know anyone who flew it who didn't fall in love with it. It was a good, safe airplane."

Lloyd Griffin
B-47 pilot

A B-47 pilot communicates with ground crew before takeoff. The airplane's remarkable range meant that it could get from U.S. bases to virtually anywhere in the world.

Engineers realized that the shape of swept wings was more efficient than traditional straight wings, allowing the jet to get more speed out of its power.

swept wing: A wing that is angled back on either side, creating a roughly triangular shape.

Centurion Tank

A prototype for the British Centurion tank had been made during World War II, but combat models were not ready until after the war. During the Cold War, the Centurion was used by armies worldwide. It was fast and mobile. However, it had the **firepower** of a heavy tank. The combination helped keep the Centurion in production until the 1990s.

The main gun of the Centurion was originally a 17-pounder (76-mm) gun. It later became the more powerful L7 105-mm gun.

firepower: The amount of offensive weapons, such as guns or cannon, a vehicle possesses.

HEAVY GUNS

Tanks played an important role in frontline **maneuvers**. They were constantly being upgraded. The Centurion's guns became bigger and its armor became thicker. Tasks such as aiming at a target became computerized.

T-64 TANK

The main Soviet response to Western tanks was the T-64 medium tank, which appeared in 1966. It was well armored. Its innovations included an automatic loader for its 125-mm gun; that meant one fewer crew member in its cramped cabin! The T-64 became the basis of modern Soviet tanks.

The Centurion was used in many smaller military clashes in the Cold War. British troops used it in the Korean War (1950–1953), while Israel used it in conflicts with Soviet-backed Arab states in the 1960s and 1970s. The Centurion was such a successful main battle tank that there are more versions of it than of any other main battle tank.

Centurions firing at night use tracer shells coated with chemicals that glow to show their path in the dark.

maneuvers: The coordinated positioning and moving around of military forces.

Cruise Missile

During the Cold War, missiles became very important weapons. Missiles had been developed by Germany during World War II. These "flying bombs" were not very accurate and had a short range. However, during the Cold War, there were great advances in missile technology. A cruise missile is any kind of self-propelled bomb that can fly—"cruise"—under its own power. It has three key parts: a **guidance system**, a warhead, and a propulsion system.

Flames blaze as a cruise missile is fired from the deck of a U.S. warship. The missiles can be fired from land, from the air, from a surface ship, or from a submerged submarine.

guidance system: The part of a missile that steers it toward the target.

A NEW THREAT

The cruise missile could travel at sub or **supersonic** speeds and strike at short or very long range. It could carry conventional or nuclear bombs. Later missiles could be steered to their targets by a computer. Others hugged the shape of the landscape as they flew just above it.

POWER BLOCS

During the Cold War, many nations joined alliances for greater security. The United States and its European allies formed the North Atlantic Treaty Organization (NATO). In response, the Soviet Union and its allies formed an alliance called the Warsaw Pact.

The U.S. Army's first surface-to-surface cruise missile was the MGM-1 Matador. It was based in Germany during the Cold War. It was capable of striking any of the countries in the Warsaw Pact.

A missile blasts a warehouse during an exercise. The missiles are usually aimed at "high value" targets, such as ships, transportation links, or command and control centers.

A **Tomahawk** cruise missile flies above mountains in California shortly after being launched in 1980.

supersonic: Traveling faster than the speed of sound: 768 miles per hour (1,236 km/h).

More than 5,000 Phantoms were built in various models before production ended in 1979.

F-4 Phantom

One of the most successful warplanes ever built entered service in 1961. This was the F-4 Phantom. This **twin-seat** fighter–bomber could carry many different weapons, including nuclear missiles. As a bomber, Phantoms worked in teams of two. As a fighter aircraft, Phantoms flown by the U.S. or its allies were more than a match for any of the Soviet-made MiG aircraft that they met.

EYEWITNESS

"I only have to think Speed, and I am at 600 knots in seconds. Think Height and I am gazing down from an eight-mile-high perch within one minute."

Robert Prest
RAF Fighter Pilot

twin-seat: An aircraft with two cockpits, both of which have the full range of controls.

OUTSTANDING PERFORMANCE

The Phantom is still in use today, thanks to its technical abilities. The supersonic airplane can fly at twice the speed of sound, or Mach 2: over 1,600 mph (2,575 km/h). It can fly at an **altitude** of 60,000 feet (18,288 m) and has a range of 1,300 miles (2,090 km). It has broken world records for the highest and fastest flights.

The Phantom carries more than 18,000 pounds (8,165 kg) of weapons. It tracks targets using its Pave Tack system. The Pave Tack is carried in a pod beneath the aircraft. It uses laser and infrared to designate targets for the weapons and to guide them onto their target.

During an exercise, a policeman in chemical warfare clothing guards an F-4 Phantom. The pilot sits in the front cockpit, with a weapons systems officer in the rear cockpit.

F-4 Phantoms fly in formation with F-15 Eagles during an operation in 1981.

altitude: The height above the ground at which an airplane flies.

These F-15s are armed with Sidewinder and AIM-7 Sparrow missiles carried on the pylons beneath their wings.

F-15 Eagle

The F-15 Eagle is the world's most successful fighter jet. It was designed to outfly any Russian-made aircraft. Flown in battle by American and Israeli pilots, its record of **air-to-air combat** "kills" was an amazing 104–0. For more than 30 years, it was the king of the skies. Its pilots were all impressed by how easy it was to maneuver and to fly in action.

 air-to-air combat: Fighting between two aircraft in flight.

A SUPER JET

The Eagle entered U.S. Air Force service in 1976. It was the most advanced fighter of its day. It could scare away enemy aircraft to win control of the skies.

EYEWITNESS

"The Eagle is an absolute joy to fly, easy and forgiving, a fact which doesn't change even when flying it aggressively."

Lt Col Michael Shower
Commander, 90th Fighter Squadron

The Eagle's powerful engines allowed the plane to take off almost vertically. Its wings were bigger than on most fast jets. That gave the pilot more maneuverability. The cockpit was full of new technology, like the hands-on throttle and stick (HOTAS). Buttons on the **joystick** allowed the pilot to control weapons and other systems without letting go of the stick.

The thrust of the F-15's twin engines is far greater than its weight, enabling it to accelerate into a vertical climb.

joystick: The column that controls the height and direction of an airplane.

F-86 Sabre

Early in the Cold War, the Sabre became a firm a favorite of U.S. Air Force pilots. It was another swept-wing aircraft. At the end of World War II (1939–1945), the Americans had seized German experimental information. This showed that a swept wing gave great stability at high speeds. The Sabre saw heavy combat during the Korean War (1950–1953). It operated as a **fighter-bomber**.

The Sabre is the most produced of all Western jet fighters: 9,860 planes were built.

fighter-bomber: An airplane that can attack other aircraft in the air or targets on the ground.

Lieutenant Colonel Richard F. Turner was one of the **aces** of the 4th Fighter Interceptor Wing in Korea.

A restored Sabre banks into a turn during an air display.

KOREAN VICTOR

The war in Korea saw the last major air battles in warfare. Later in the Cold War, air-to-air missiles took over. The Sabre's record against Soviet MiGs in Korea was outstanding. For every Sabre that was downed, seven MiGs were shot down.

The Sabre had a top speed of 675 miles per hour (1,085 km/h) and it reached an altitude of 48,300 feet (14,722 m). It was fast and easy to maneuver, and it was armed with six machine guns.

EYEWITNESS

"[The F-86 Sabre is] so easy to fly you can almost control it with your thoughts."

Sabre test pilot

ace: A pilot who has shot down a certain number of enemy aircraft.

The Harrier took just 2 minutes 22 seconds to fly to an altitude of 40,000 feet (12,200 m) from vertical takeoff.

Harrier

For years, engineers had tried to design a jet aircraft that could rise vertically into the air rather than needing a long runway. Finally, they succeeded when the Harrier came into operation with Britain's Royal Air Force (RAF) in 1969. This **fixed-wing** vertical take-off and landing (VTOL) strike-fighter rose from the ground like a helicopter. Then it flew into action as a conventional jet.

fixed wing: Wings that remain in one position, unlike the rotating blades of a helicopter.

Harriers come in to land on a carrier. They were armed with 30mm guns and carried bombs and rockets.

ROTATING ENGINES

Helicopters and jets use rotors or direct thrust, respectively, to take off. The Harrier's Pegasus engine had four nozzles that could rotate. To take off or land, they swung into a vertical position. A VTOL aircraft did not need a runway. That made it very flexible. It could be launched from small airfields or **aircraft carriers**. A special carrier version, the Sea Harrier, was launched in 1980. It fought in the Falklands War between Britain and Argentina in 1982. It shot down 20 enemy jets in return for one Harrier lost.

EYEWITNESS

"It required all the skill that I could bring to bear in terms of handling the aeroplane. That's what test flying was like in the 1960s—there were no simulators."

John Farley
Original RAF test pilot, 1964

Sea Harriers wait to take off from an aircraft carrier during the Falklands War.

aircraft carrier: A warship with a flat deck to allow airplanes to take off and land.

English Electric Lightning

In 1958, a British-made **interceptor** reached twice the speed of sound: Mach 2. This speed that earned the airplane the "Lightning" name made it a key part of Cold War defenses in Europe. Pilots said that flying this plane was like being strapped to a rocket.

The Lightning was the first airplane capable of "supercruise," or spending long periods at supersonic speeds.

interceptor: A fighter that can interrupt the flight of an enemy aircraft.

Air enthusiasts watch a Lightning take off in the 1960s, armed with air-to-air missiles.

RAPID CLIMBER

The Lightning could also climb to altitude super fast. After takeoff, it could shoot up almost vertically. It could reach 40,000 feet (12,200 m) in just two minutes. Such power used a lot of fuel, so the airplane's range was short. At supersonic speed, it could only fly for 850 miles (1,370 km). Its wings were swept back to allow it to accelerate so enormously fast.

The "racehorse of the skies" was popular. Pilots loved to fly it. During the Cold War, it was **scrambled** in order to turn back Soviet reconnaissance aircraft that were headed for Great Britain. A total of 337 Lightnings were built. However, despite its popularity, the aircraft turned out to be the last British supersonic fighter to be manufactured.

EYEWITNESS

"For the pure joy of flying, the Lightning still heads the list. It was and ideed still is a magnificent aircraft, and a credit to the designers and test pilots who developed and brought it into service for people like me to enjoy."

Brian Carroll
Wing Commander, RAF

scramble: To get pilots into aircraft and the aircraft off the ground very quickly.

The USS *City of Corpus Christi* cruises on the surface; the Los Angeles-class submarines can travel at speeds of 20 knots (23 miles per hour; 37 km/h).

Los Angeles Class Submarine

With many uses and well engineered, the Los Angeles class is still the backbone of the U.S. Navy. The vessels in this class of nuclear-powered **fast-attack** submarines were built from 1972 to 1996. As of 2022, 26 were still in service. Their top speed is believed to be 30 to 33 knots (35 to 38 mph). They can attack enemy land targets up to 1,550 miles (2,500 km) away using Tomahawk missiles.

fast-attack: A type of submarine designed to strike at enemy vessels.

SUB HUNTER

Los Angeles class vessels were designed to have other functions. One of the most important was to protect aircraft carriers and other warships from enemy submarines. They use radar to track enemy vessels and **torpedoes** to attack and destroy them.

In addition to its fighting capacity, these subs have many other uses. They can gather intelligence, deliver Special Forces to remote places, lay mines, and carry out search-and-rescue missions. They can even stay beneath the polar ice caps for 90 days.

EYEWITNESS

"Our biggest threat is another submarine. Our best defense against enemy subs will be tactics, training, and motivation. The crew that acts first and makes the fewest mistakes will win."

Executive Officer
U.S. Los Angeles class sub

The crew of a new Los Angeles class submarine stands at attention on its superstructure as it is launched down a slipway into the water.

The command deck of a Los Angeles submarine is cramped. So is the whole vessel; there are 129 people on board.

torpedo: An underwater missile that has its own engine to push it through the water.

The M1 Abrams had a crew of four: commander, driver, loader, and gunner.

M1 Abrams

The Soviet Union and the United States, the two **superpowers** of the Cold War, were in a technological arms race. A major area of this competition was in tank technology. Tanks became heavier as their armor got thicker and their guns got larger. The M-1 Abrams entered service in 1980 as the main battle tank of the U.S. Army and the Marine Corps. It was the most advanced tank of the period.

superpowers: The countries that led the Cold War—the United States and the Soviet Union.

A POPULAR GUN

The M1 was covered in **laminate** Chobam armor to protect it from a new battlefield threat: missiles. The M1 carried a 105mm main gun with a kill range of 8,200 feet (2,500 m). That was much further than its Soviet counterpart. The U.S. tank could hit the enemy before it was within the enemy's range. Its acceleration and top speed were also superior to enemy tanks.

EYEWITNESS

"She'll do about 50 miles per hour [80 km/h] wide open. And that's with the governor on. Without the speed control we've hit 70 miles per hour [110 km/h]!"

Floyd Miller
M1 driver, Fort Knox

A fire-control computer calculated the range of the target and the angle of fire so that its shells were fired as accurately as possible.

A member of an M1 Abrams crew keeps watch with the .50 caliber (12.7mm) heavy machine gun that is the tank's usual secondary armament.

laminate: A hard material made by combining thin layers of metal and ceramic.

Ship's personnel "man the rails" of the USS *Nimitz* as it is towed from port, ready to begin a mission.

USS *Nimitz*

The largest and most powerful warships ever built are the Nimitz **class** super-carriers. There were 10 of these nuclear-powered aircraft carriers built in the mid-1970s. On the Nimitz class, the flight deck is 1,092 feet (333 m) long and 252 feet (79 m) wide. This enormous take-off space was necessary because aircraft were getting bigger and heavier. These carriers can carry as many as 90 aircraft. They are the size of a small town. The ships have a crew of more than 5,000 people.

class: A group of warships that are all based on the same design and specifications.

MULTITASKER

The first carrier in the class, USS *Nimitz*, was deployed to the Indian Ocean in 1980. Radicals in Iran had taken U.S. personnel **hostage** in the capital, Tehran. The ship filled the role of a floating airbase during the crisis. The carriers are used to carry out sea and air blockades, to make missile strikes, and to lay minefields.

Nimitz-class vessels can stay at sea for an amazing 13 years. They run on nuclear power, so they do not need to refuel. They just need supply ships to bring provisions for the crew. The USS *Dwight D. Eisenhower* set a record in 1980 by staying at sea for 152 days without once visiting port.

FLOATING TOWN

A Nimitz-class carrier is like a small town. Its cooks serve up to 20,000 meals a day. The barber trims 1,500 heads a week. There's a 53-bed hospital on board, and one multi-faith chapel. Fresh water is distilled every day and the ship carries food supplies for up to 10 weeks.

Sea Stallion helicopters are stored in a hangar beneath the deck of USS *Nimitz*; the helicopters' rotors fold to make them fit better.

This aerial photograph shows the USS *Nimitz* underway, with aircraft arranged around its flight deck.

hostage: Someone who is held against their will for a particular purpose.

Nuclear Bomb

Atomic bombs, or nuclear bombs, were often referred to as "the bomb." They dominated the thinking of all nations during the Cold War. People were terrified of what would happen if there was a nuclear war. The United States and the Soviet Union spent billions of dollars in a nuclear arms race. Everyone hoped a war would not begin by accident.

A mushroom cloud rises from a test atomic explosion. The cloud is formed by a mass of hot, rising gases.

atomic: A bomb that releases huge power by fusing atoms together or splitting them apart.

MUTUALLY ASSURED DESTRUCTION

Both superpowers built enough nuclear weapons to obliterate the other. Politicians and military commanders argued that the best way to stop the enemy from launching an atomic strike was to have a huge nuclear **arsenal**. If the enemy struck, it would bring a nuclear strike in return that would destroy it. This was called mutually assured destruction.

By the 1980s, there were so many bombs that the two superpowers agreed to reduce their nuclear arsenals to make the world safer. The two bombs dropped on Japan remain the only nuclear bombs ever used in warfare.

EYEWITNESS

"No issue carries more importance to the long-term health and security of humanity than the effort to reduce and, perhaps one day, rid the world of nuclear weapons."

Lawrence M. Krauss
Professor of Physics

Titan missiles, stored in deep underground bunkers in the United States, were the main U.S. nuclear threat from 1962 to 1965.

An atomic cannon is tested in 1953. It was intended to fire short-range nuclear missiles but was never used in battle.

arsenal: A collection of weapons or a place where weapons are stored.

Polaris

Early in the Cold War, the U.S. military had relied on aircraft to carry and launch nuclear warheads. Later, it decided to give more importance to missiles. To make them difficult to detect, the authorities ordered a class of new submarines that would carry many of the long-range **strategic** missiles. Special submarines were developed to carry the missiles. Together, they were all known as "boomers."

EYEWITNESS

"The Polaris firing I witnessed was a most satisfying and fascinating experience. It is still incredible to me that a missile can be successfully and accurately fired from beneath the sea."

John F. Kennedy
U.S. President, in 1963

USS *George Washington* sails on the surface while on patrol.

strategic: Related to the overall aims of a war or campaign, not to the immediate action.

UNDERWATER

The first of these ballistic weapons was the Polaris A1 missile. The A1 had a range of 2,500 miles (4,600 km) and could fly at up to 8,000 miles per hour (13,000 km/h). The British and Spanish let U.S. submarines use their ports. That brought the Soviet Union within range. The missiles were a key part of the **deterrence** against a Soviet attack.

The USS *George Washington* was one of the first Polaris submarines. It carried 12 Polaris A1s. Between 1960 and 1966, the U.S. Navy launched 41 boomers, sometimes called the "forty-one for freedom." All the subs were named after heroes from U.S. history.

A Polaris A3 missile is launched from the submerged submarine SSBN *Robert E. Lee*. The A3 replaced the A1 in 1963.

deterrence: Preventing an enemy attack by threatening an even bigger attack in return.

Resolution Class Submarine

The British built four nuclear-powered submarines in the Resolution class. They enabled the British to fire nuclear missiles at the Soviet Union if they were ever attacked. These submarines in the Resolution class replaced aircraft as Britain's major nuclear deterrent. Key to their operations was that the U.S. government allowed its British **allies** to carry American Polaris ballistic missiles.

HMS *Renown*, one of the four Resolution class subs, prepares to dive. Each of the vessels carried a complement of 143 people, divided into two complete crews.

allies: Countries that cooperate with one another for defense against a shared enemy.

UNDERWATER

The Resolution submarines patrolled the seas, watching enemy subs without being detected themselves. That meant they had to stay underwater for long periods. Their engines also had to be very quiet so their presence was not picked up by enemy **sonar**. The subs patrolled 24/7, so each vessel carried two complete crews, known as Port and Starboard. The vessels were on a permanent state of alert, so they were always ready to launch a missile.

The Resolution class resembled the U.S. Lafayette class. It was designed to carry 16 A-3 Polaris missiles. Its top speed when submerged was 28.5 miles per hour (46 km/h). The Resolution class was taken out of service in 1994, when the Trident missile took over from Polaris.

Crew members stand on the deck of HMS *Resolution* during a rendezvous with a British helicopter during an exercise.

RUNNING LATE

HMS *Resolution* fired its first Polaris missile in 1968. It was part of Demonstration and Shakedown Operations (DASO). DASO is a series of tests that make sure a vessel and crew are working well. *Resolution* passed, but the missile was launched 15 milliseconds behind schedule.

sonar: A system that locates an underwater enemy by detecting sound waves.

Fylingdales in northern England is a radar station set up to detect early signs of a Soviet ballistic missile attack on Europe.

Spy Satellites

Getting warnings of enemy plans or activities became very important during the Cold War. Both sides used secret agents and had listening posts that deciphered enemy radio transmissions. U.S. spy **satellites** that looked down on enemy territory from space became a crucial source of information.

satellite: An artificial device put into orbit at very high altitudes around Earth.

THE HEXAGON PROGRAM

The Hexagon satellite program was nicknamed Big Bird. Between 1971 and 1986, 20 satellites were put into orbit. They carried super high-resolution cameras that took images of the Soviet Union, China, or any other enemy.

The film from the camera was dropped in **re-entry vehicles** and retrieved in mid-air by U.S. aircraft. The images were then taken to be analyzed. All this was done without the help of computers. This Hexagon program was the most successful spy satellite program of the Cold War.

EYEWITNESS

"I thought they were crazy. They envisaged a satellite... supplying film at speeds of 200 inches (5 m) per second. The precision and complexity blew my mind."

Joseph Prusak
Engineer, Hexagon Project

This photo from a spy satellite shows a Russian Typhoon class submarine at a quayside. Analysts learned how to decipher the aerial images with great accuracy.

Modern satellites are usually used for communications purposes, such as transmitting TV signals.

re-entry vehicle: A craft designed to re-enter Earth's atmosphere from space.

SR-71 Blackbird

The Blackbird was a revolutionary aircraft. It was the world's fastest jet. It could fly at Mach 3: three times the speed of sound, or 2,485 miles per hour (4,000 km/h). It flew 16 miles (25.75 km) above the Earth, on the edge of the **atmosphere**. This was so high that the crew had to wear spacesuits.

Everything about the SR-71 was designed to make it invisible to enemy radar.

atmosphere: The layer of gases that surrounds Earth and stretches out toward space.

Technicians prepare an SR-71 for a mission. The undercarriage of the SR-71 was the largest titanium object ever made.

REVOLUTIONARY AIRPLANE

The Blackbird even looked different from other aircraft. Its shape was one of the first examples of "stealth technology." It was designed so that radar signals would not bounce off it and give it away. The black paint that gave the aircraft its name also helped reduce its radar profile. The paint was specially made to get rid of excess heat. Friction caused the exterior to heat up to 392°F (200°C).

The Blackbird was made of titanium and **composite** materials. The United States didn't have enough titanium and had to buy it from its enemy, the Soviet Union. The jet used special fuel, so its engines were specially designed and it had its own fleet of tankers.

EYEWITNESS

"The SR-71...stands alone as a significant contributor to Cold War victory and as the fastest plane ever—and only 93 Air Force pilots ever steered the 'sled,' as we called our aircraft...I loved that jet."

Brian Shul
Major, United States Air Force

composite: A material made by combining other materials, such as plastics.

Strategic Defense Initiative

Defending the United States against missile attack was a problem no one thought could be solved. In March 1983, however, U.S. president Ronald Reagan announced the Strategic Defense Initiative (SDI). This aimed to build a defense shield in space to intercept incoming missiles. The program was highly ambitious: None of the technology required existed at the time. The public soon called it "Star Wars."

A Delta II rocket lifts off in 1989 carrying equipment for SDI tests in space.

initiative: A step that is the first part of a new program.

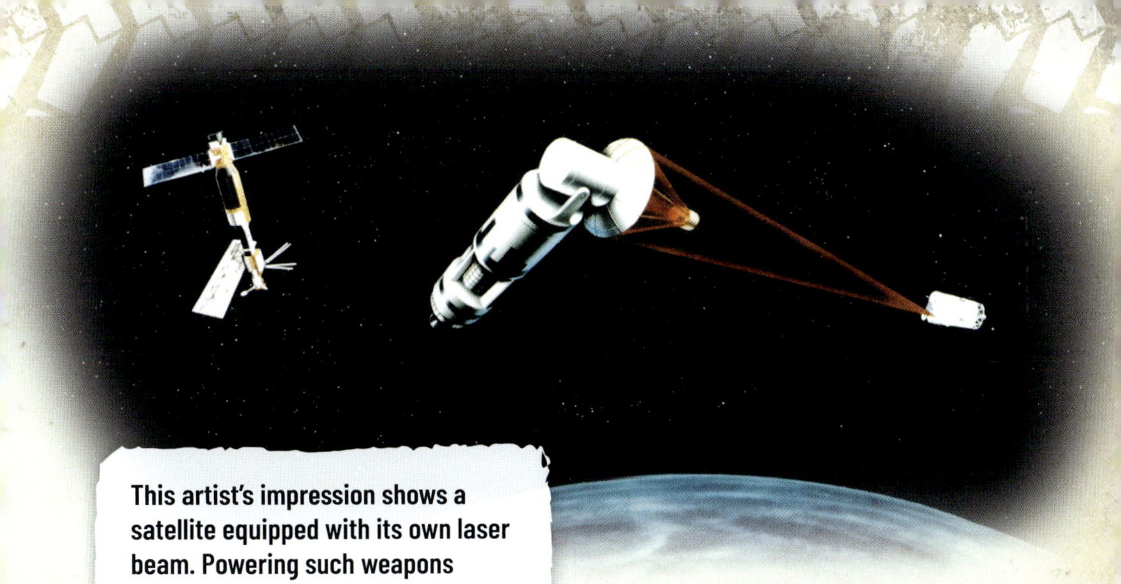

This artist's impression shows a satellite equipped with its own laser beam. Powering such weapons remained beyond scientific knowledge in the 1980s.

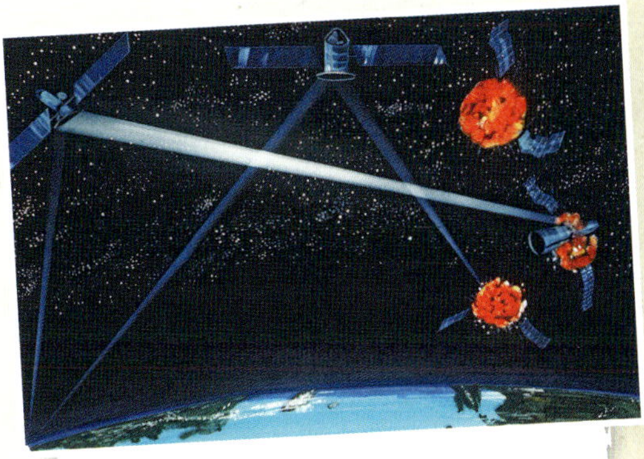

In this artist's impression, satellites use ground-based laser beams to destroy targets in space.

A SAFETY CURTAIN

The idea behind the SDI was that its satellites would detect any approaching ballistic missiles. Other satellites would then be used to destroy the missiles in midair using various types of **laser** or particle beams. No one knew if such technology could be created, or how long it might take to develop.

SDI soon ran into public opposition. It was hugely expensive at a time when the Soviet threat seemed to be falling anyway. No one even knew if it would work. After $30 billion had been spent on research, the program was quietly abandoned.

EYEWITNESS

"We seek neither military superiority nor political advantage. Our only purpose —one all people share—is to search for ways to reduce the danger of nuclear war."

Ronald Reagan
U.S. President, in 1986

laser: A highly concentrated beam of light.

Trident

The Trident program was the third generation in the U.S. **ballistic missile** program. It followed the Polaris and Poseidon programs. The first Trident I was launched in 1979, and Trident missiles were carried on the U.S. Navy's Ohio-class submarines. The Trident I was replaced by Trident II in 2005.

A Trident lifts off during tests in 1978. It was destroyed seconds later when its guidance system went wrong.

EYEWITNESS

"We're a friendly group of guys. We have to be; we do a lot of work in a very tight place."

Missile technician
Trident submarine

ballistic missile: A missile that is initially self powered but then falls to its target by use of gravity.

DESTRUCTIVE POWER

Trident I was a very powerful nuclear missile. Each of its **warheads** had eight times the destructive power of the nuclear bomb that destroyed the Japanese city of Hiroshima in 1945.

With a longer range, Trident was a big advance on the Poseidons it replaced. The submarines that carried Trident were also bigger than Polaris Poseidon subs; they could patrol an area 10 times as large. Trident I was launched from deep below the ocean's surface to the edge of space. In space, computers would then guide the missile to its destination.

A Trident II missile is launched during tests in 1987. Each missile can carry up to 12 nuclear warheads.

The open missile tubes of the nuclear-powered ballistic missile submarine Ohio. Each one holds a Trident missile.

warhead: The part of a missile that carries the explosive charge.

The U-2 was designed to fly so high that it was out of range of Soviet anti-aircraft fire, but it never managed to do so.

U-2

The U-2 spy plane was first launched in 1955. It was intended to be able to overfly the Soviet Union for military **reconnaissance** and use powerful cameras to take photographs that would give information on Soviet military deployment. Its pilots did not enjoy flying it. They nicknamed the aircraft the "dragon lady" because they said that it was hard to fly and even harder to land. The U-2 had long, narrow wings and could fly at an altitude of 70,000 feet (21,336 m).

EYEWITNESS

"I was a pilot flying an airplane and it just so happened that where I was flying made what I was doing spying."

Gary F. Powers
Pilot of downed U-2

reconnaissance: Gathering information about enemy armed forces and movements.

Gary Powers was captured by the Soviets. The U.S. pilot was put on trial and forced to confess to being on a spying mission.

Russians examine the wreckage of the U-2 shot down on May 1, 1960. The Soviet Union used the plane for propaganda.

BALANCING ACT

The plane's design is based on that of a **glider**. There is little room for the pilot. He has to wear a spacesuit to fly so high to keep him from getting sick. The plane's balance is so sensitive that film for its camera has to be carefully positioned.

The U-2 entered service in 1957, but the Americans kept its existence secret. The "U" stood for "utility." The name didn't really mean anything, in case the Soviets heard people talking about it. However, on May 1, 1960, a U-2 was shot down over Soviet territory. The United States denied it even existed, but the Soviets had captured the pilot, so they had proof.

glider: An airplane that does not have an engine and flies using rising currents of air.

A Vulcan takes off. Its delta wings gave it great stability at high speeds.

Vulcan Bomber

The British Vulcan bomber had a number of roles during the Cold War. It carried nuclear weapons and could threaten a strike on the Soviet Union. Two Vulcans were kept ready at all times, with their engines running and the pilots onboard, in order to intercept any missile strike on Britain. The Vulcans had just four minutes to get in the air and shoot the missiles down before they reached their targets!

EYEWITNESS

"When we watched the [Vulcans] roll down the runway and roar off into the sky we did not know where they were going. Back to base—or a one-way ride to Moscow?"

Peter Noyle
Technician, Bristol Siddeley Engines

intercept: To stop someone or something from reaching a destination.

VARIOUS DUTIES

If the Vulcan had to intercept a missile, it would do so from an altitude of 50,000 feet (15,240 m) at a range of 100–200 miles (160–320 km). Once it had fired its own missile, the Vulcan would flee as fast as possible. However, the chances of the pilots escaping were slim.

The Vulcan had other tasks, too. It was part of Britain's nuclear deterrent. The delta-wing jet acted as a strategic bomber that could carry both nuclear and conventional weapons. The Vulcan flew at super-high altitudes, out of range of enemy radar or missiles. It was painted white because experts thought that gave it better **camouflage** at high altitudes.

The probe on the nose of the Vulcan was used for midair refueling when it was attached to a hose from another airplane.

Two Vulcans fly above the radar station at Fylingdales, in northern England, which would give them warning of a missile attack.

camouflage: Color schemes designed to make something more difficult to see.

Glossary

ace: A pilot who has shot down a certain number of enemy aircraft.

arsenal: A collection of weapons or a place where weapons are stored.

atomic: A bomb that releases huge power by fusing atoms together or splitting them apart.

ballistic missile: A missile that is initially self-powered but then falls to its target by use of gravity.

camouflage: Color schemes designed to make an object more difficult to see.

class: A group of warships that are all based on the same design and specifications.

composite: A material made by combining other materials, such as plastics.

deterrence: Preventing an enemy attack by threatening an even bigger attack in return.

fallout: The spread of harmful microscopic nuclear material after an atomic explosion.

fast-attack: A type of submarine designed to strike at enemy vessels.

glider: An airplane that does not have an engine and flies using rising currents of air.

ideology: A system of political ideas that forms the basis of a society.

interceptor: A fighter that can interrupt the flight of an enemy aircraft.

joystick: The column that controls the height and direction of an airplane.

laser: A highly concentrated beam of light.

maneuvers: The coordinated positioning and moving around of military forces.

nuclear: A bomb that works by releasing the vast power contained in atoms.

reconnaissance: Gathering information about enemy armed forces and movements.

scramble: To get pilots into aircraft and the aircraft off the ground very quickly.

strategic: Related to the overall aims of a war or campaign, not to the immediate action.

superpowers: The countries that led the Cold War: the United States and the Soviet Union.

supersonic: Traveling faster than the speed of sound: 768 miles per hour (1,236 km/h).

swept wing: A wing that is angled back, rather than sticking straight out.

torpedo: An underwater missile that has its own engine to push it through the water.

warhead: The part of a missile that carries the explosive charge.

Further Information

Cooke, Tim. *A Timeline of Guns, Missiles, and Rockets.* Capstone, 2018.

Ransom, Candice. *How Aircraft Carriers Work.* Lerner Publishing, 2020.

Ripley, Tim. *Torpedoes, Missiles and Cannons: Physics Goes to War.* Lerner Publishing, 2018

Sheinkin, Steve. *Fallout: Spies, Superbombs and the Ultimate Cold War Showdown.* Roaring Brook Press, 2021.

Ware, Pat. *Inside the Cold War (Geek's Guide).* Rosen Publishing, 2019.

Websites

https://coldwar.unc.edu/
This collection of visual assets about the Cold war includes cartoons and posters.

http://www.shoppbs.pbs.org/wgbh/amex/bomb/index.
PBS's website deals with the race to build ever more destructive weapons.

https://www.ducksters.com/history/cold_war/summary.php
This site for younger students gives quick information on a variety of Cold War topics.

https://www.history.com/topics/cold-war/cold-war-history
This website gives a general chronological overview of the Cold War.

Publisher's note to educators and parents: Our editors have carefully reviewed these websites to ensure that they are suitable for students. Many websites change frequently, however, and we cannot guarantee that a site's future contents will continue to meet our high standards of quality and educational value. Be advised that students should be closely supervised whenever they access the Internet.

Index